Lily's Little Cajun Cookbook

Cajun Recipes and Southern Stories

By Eric Wilder

All rights reserved. No part of this book may be reproduced, stored in a retrieval system, or transmitted in any form, or by any means without the prior written permission of the author, except by a reviewer who may quote brief passages in a review to be printed in a newspaper, magazine, journal website or blog.

© 2010 by Gary Pittenger

First Edition

ISBN:978-0-9791165-2-0
Published by Gondwana Press
Edmond, Oklahoma

For Marilyn

Contents

Introduction	6
Lily's Crab Balls	8
Lily's Cajun Coffee	10
Lily's Tomatoes Bonaparte	12
Lily's Mirliton Dressing	14
Nutrias, Yashicas and Steaming Pots of Gumbo	16
Lily's Filé Gumbo	18
Lily's Sausage, Tomato and Okra Gumbo	20
A Mardi Gras to Remember—or Maybe Forget	22
Dr. M's Cattle Ranch	24
Lily's Squash and Sausage Casserole	26
Lily's Seafood Stock	28
Lily's Oyster Stew	29
Lily's Oyster Dressing	31
Lily's Steamed Oysters	33
Midnight on the Bayou	35
Lily's Dirty Rice Dressing	38
Riding Rodan	40
Lily's Crawfish Pie	43
Lily's Crawfish Etouffee	45
A Knight at the Ball	47
Lily's Beignets	50
Lily's Bread Pudding with Rum Sauce	52

Raining Cats and Dogs	54
Lily's Barbecue Shrimp	56
Prince of Arabi	58
Lily's Chicken Sauce Piquante	60
Clueless in Chalmette	62
Lily's Chalmette Meatloaf	64
Lily's Rice Dressing	66
Lily's Red Fish Chalmette	68
Lily's Cajun Butter	70
Lily's Famous Eggplant Dressing	72
Harvey's Diet Tip	74
Culture, Cuisine, Hurricanes and Oil Spills	76

Eric Wilder

Introduction

For those of you married more than once, you already know how hard it is to keep a relationship working well. Often, it is impossible. When my first marriage with then wife Gail failed after seven years, I felt I was losing more than a life-partner; I was also losing her entire family. I'll explain.

While Gail and I are both from Louisiana, she grew up south of New Orleans, I north of Shreveport. This probably doesn't mean much to those from other states, but everything for Louisianans. The French and Spanish originally populated New Orleans and most of south Louisiana. English speaking people populated north Louisiana. Catholicism is the dominant religion of south Louisiana; Protestantism predominates in north Louisiana. While my mother was a wonderful cook, as were my grandmothers, I grew up eating cornbread, pork chops and fried potatoes. I wasn't introduced to the wonderful regional Cajun and Creole cuisine of south Louisiana until I began dating Gail and met her mother Lily.

Lily was the quintessential Cajun cook. She knew every dish she prepared by heart, always using just the right amount of spice or Creole seasoning. I soon became

Lily's Little Cajun Cookbook

a connoisseur of gumbo, learning no two bowlfuls are ever quite the same. While I have now tasted many bowls of the wonderful concoction—a dish I like to call "Nectar of the Gods"— prepared by cooks and chefs alike, I have never tasted any that quite compares to my former mother-in-law Lily's. While I lost Lily along with many other things in my divorce, I will always remember her as the greatest Cajun/Creole cook I have ever known. This little Cajun cookbook is my feeble attempt to immortalize her culinary greatness.

Lily's Crab Balls

Lily not only loved to cook, she also loved to entertain. Here is a recipe for one of her favorite appetizers, and also one of mine.

Ingredients

- 14 oz. crabmeat
- 2 cups bread crumbs, dry
- 2 tablespoons lemon juice, fresh
- 2 tablespoons onion, finely minced
- 1 tablespoon mustard, dry
- ½ cup white wine, dry
- 1 pound bacon

Directions

Remove shell and cartilage from crab meat. In medium bowl, combine crabmeat, bread crumbs, lemon juice, minced onion, mustard, and enough wine to moisten the mixture. Mix thoroughly and shape into quarter-sized balls. Wrap crabmeat balls in a half slice of bacon, covering crab mixture completely. Secure with toothpicks. Place in oven and broil for about fifteen minutes, turning frequently, until bacon is crispy on all sides. Enjoy.

Eric Wilder

Lily's Cajun Coffee

Gail grew up in Chalmette, a city south of New Orleans devastated by Hurricanes Katrina and Rita. While attending college in Monroe, she and I would often leave at night from our respective menial jobs and drive to Chalmette for the weekend. We would enter the old wood-framed structure quietly and sleep in one of the empty bedrooms in back. At five, our nightly rest always ended along with the booming bass voice of a distant cousin named Admiral.

"Hey Harvey, you and Lily gonna sleep all morning?" he would bellow.

Gail's parents, Lily and Harvey were already awake, although barely, and Lily would open the door for Admiral and let him into the kitchen. He always came in the back door. Lily would start a pot of strong coffee. She didn't use a modern coffee pot, brewing hers in a simple drip pot that she heated on the open natural gas flame of her little stove. Like many Cajuns, she employed a blend of coffee and chicory that produced a strong, aromatic brew. I still remember the aroma of Lily's Cajun coffee.

Admiral's voice was so deep and booming, it actually shook the walls. At least it felt that way after only four hours of sleep. Soon, Gail and I would succumb to the cacophony, and stories about Fats Domino we had all heard many times before. She would roll out of bed, put on her robe and tread down the hall to the kitchen. Finally, I would rub my eyes, take a big whiff of the coffee aroma wafting from the kitchen, and follow her.

Two wives later, I still love coffee, but in all my travels I have never had a cup as good as Lily brewed, or experienced that wonderful aroma that can revive you fully from a hard day's work, a long drive, and only four hours of sleep

Lily's Tomatoes Bonaparte

South Louisiana was a wild and treacherous place when first populated by the French, and later the Spanish. Those early settlers not only managed to subsist, they thrived by learning from the Indians to cook with native fruits, roots and vines. They also learned how to embellish what they created with tomatoes, one of Lily's favorite foods.

Ingredients

- 2 large Creole tomatoes
- ¼ pound fresh mozzarella cheese
- Fresh basil
- 1 teaspoon balsamic vinegar
- ¼ cup high-quality salad vinegar
- 1 teaspoon Dijon mustard
- ¾ cup extra-virgin olive oil
- ½ teaspoon salt
- Freshly ground pepper

Lily's Little Cajun Cookbook

Directions

Slice tomatoes about 1/3 inch thick. Place a slice on each of 2 salad plates, then a slice of mozzarella, then several basil leaves. Make 2 more layers and drizzle with as much dressing as desired. To make dressing, whisk the vinegar and mustard together in a small bowl. Gradually pour in the olive oil, continuously whisking. Add salt and continue whisking until smooth. After adding dressing to Bonaparte's, place a few basil leaves around the plate and grind pepper lightly over all.

Eric Wilder

Lily's Mirliton Dressing

A mirliton is a green, pear-shaped fruit found in abundance in south Louisiana. They crawled up the fence by the dozens in Lily's backyard. There are hundreds of ways to prepare this tasty plant, usually like a vegetable such as squash, but Lily especially liked this particular variation, and so do I.

Ingredients

- 8 mirlitons
- 1/4 cup liquid crab boil
- 2 large onions, chopped
- 6 tablespoons butter
- 1 cup of extra virgin olive oil
- 1 cup cheap white wine
- 1 tablespoon lemon juice
- 1 teaspoon paprika
- 1 teaspoon salt
- 2 eggs, well beaten
- 2 sprigs thyme
- 2 cups bread crumbs
- 2 cloves garlic, minced

Lily's Little Cajun Cookbook

- 1 pound crawfish tails
- 1 teaspoon black pepper
- 1 teaspoon white pepper
- 2 teaspoons chopped parsley

Directions

Simmer mirlitons about one to 1 ½ hours in salted water, or until tender. Remove from water, drain, and half. Remove the seed and scoop out pulp with a spoon. Reserve the shells. Chop the pulp and add breadcrumbs. Sauté chopped onions, garlic, and crawfish in crab boil, butter, wine, lemon juice and olive oil over medium heat until tender. Stir in pulp, salt, paprika and pepper. Stir often and cook for about 5 minutes. Add beaten eggs, parsley, and thyme. Mix thoroughly. Scoop the dressing back into the individual shells, top with breadcrumbs and dot with butter. Bake the mirlitons in a 375-degree Fahrenheit oven for 20 to 25 minutes, or until hot, and then enjoy.

Eric Wilder

Nutrias, Yashicas and Steaming Pots of Gumbo

I visited New Orleans for the first time when I was eleven. My Aunt Carmol was an elementary school teacher there, and she made sure Brother Jack and I saw every historical site, museum and park in the City. Having grown up in rural northwest Louisiana, New Orleans was the first cosmopolitan area I ever visited. It was not the last, but it remains in my mind as the most unique city in the United States and perhaps the world.

My first visit was not my last. As a college freshman, I marched in the Venus parade during Mardi Gras, experiencing Bourbon Street and the French Quarter for the first time as an adult. Most of that particular visit was spent in a drunken haze, much in the manner of college students today visiting the City and savoring Mardi Gras for the first time.

I worked in New Orleans once during summer break from college. My job title was assistant microphotographic technician seismologist. From my salary of two dollars per hour, you can tell the description was a bit overblown, but it did look good on my resume. I bought my first camera that year—a 35 mm Yashica range finder, and New Orleans provided a plethora of scenic opportunities.

Shortly after that sweltering summer I married Gail. She was from Chalmette, a city separated from New Orleans by name only. Our marriage didn't last but I learned to love her French Acadian parents, Lily and Harvey, and her entire family.

Gail had two brothers, six sisters and many aunts, uncles and cousins. Most lived less than a mile apart and all were wonderful cooks, but none better than was Gail's mother Lily. No two pots of gumbo are ever exactly alike. I know because I have consumed my fair share. Taste is subjective. That said, Lily's gumbo was the best I ever tasted and, in my opinion, the best in the world.

Harvey was a cattleman and fur buyer. During trapping season, raw fur filled the shed behind his house. He gave me a lesson once on how to grade a nutria pelt. Like calculus and religion, the lesson didn't stick. Harvey and Lily once found six-hundred dollars in cash in their deep freeze they had forgotten about. They did not have a safe and that's where they hid their cash because trappers do not take Visa or MasterCard.

Lily's Filé' Gumbo

Gumbo is probably the most characteristic dish of New Orleans and south Louisiana. Filé' gives that slippery smoothness to the dish which is so characteristic of a Gumbo. Sliced okra is used in other parts of the south to give practically the same quality but filé' belongs to Louisiana alone. Filé' is a powder made originally by Choctaw Indians from young tender sassafras leaves. There are many gumbo variations, this one made with filé' and with oysters.

Ingredients

- 1 4-pound stewing chicken
- 1 cup shucked oysters, undrained
- Salt, pepper, cayenne
- 2 quarts water
- ½ chili pepper, chopped fine
- ½ pound ham, cubed
- 2 tablespoons filé' powder
- 2 onions, chopped
- 2 cups cooked rice
- 1/8 teaspoon thyme

Lily's Little Cajun Cookbook

Directions

Cut chicken in serving portions and simmer in salted water until tender. Remove bones and cut meat in cubes. Fry ham. Brown onions in ham fat. Combine chicken, ham, onions and oyster liquor. Cover with boiling chicken stock; add salt, pepper, cayenne and chili pepper: simmer for 2 hours. About 10 minutes before serving, add oysters and just before serving moisten file´ with a little of the soup and add to remaining soup. Do not cook after adding file´. Place a mound of cooked rice in each soup plate and serve the gumbo over it

Lily's Sausage, Tomato and Okra Gumbo

Yes, there are as many different variations of gumbo as cooks that prepare it. Lily cooked them all and she usually had a pot simmering on her old stove. In fact, Gail and I counted on it. This recipe is one of her standards—a simple concoction of okra, tomato and sausage. Try it and I think you will agree that it is quite wonderful.

Ingredients

- 1 ½ pounds okra
- 1 pound tomatoes
- 2 tablespoons vegetable oil
- 2 tablespoons flour
- 1 medium onion, chopped
- 2 cloves garlic, minced
- ½ cup water
- ¼ lb andouille sausage
- ¼ teaspoon salt
- ¼ teaspoon Creole seasoning
- Cracked pepper

Lily's Little Cajun Cookbook

- ½ teaspoon sugar

Directions

Wash okra and dry. Remove stems. Slice pods into ½ inch cylinders. Peel tomatoes and chop. Heat oil in a medium saucepan and add flour. Over medium heat, make a brown roux, stirring constantly. Add onions and garlic and cook until soft. Add water, okra, tomatoes, sausage, salt, pepper, Creole seasoning and sugar. Cover and simmer over low heat for about 30 minutes. Adjust seasonings to taste. Enjoy.

A Mardi Gras to Remember, or Maybe Forget

    I was in my last semester of graduate school at the University of Arkansas. Our best friends, Toni and Terrence went with us to Chalmette to celebrate Mardi Gras. Terrence was an animal husbandry major so we spent a day and night in Vidalia, Louisiana where Gail's father, at the time, was the supervisor of a large cattle ranch. We enjoyed a personal tour of the ranch and some of Lily's gumbo before heading to Chalmette.

    Gail had a large family and once in Chalmette, each regaled us with drinks, dinners and frivolity, leading up to Mardi Gras Day. My favorite relatives were probably Junior, Lily's little brother, his gorgeous wife Joyce and pretty daughter Kim. Junior had a fishing boat and would always return from the bayou with a bounty of crab, shrimp and redfish.

    That Tuesday morning we awoke early and headed downtown. Drinking on the street was legal and we began imbibing by ten in the morning. We watched every parade we could get to. Along the way, we continued drinking.

Lily's Little Cajun Cookbook

We attempted to pace ourselves, eating hot dogs and gumbo from various street vendors. All we really succeeded in doing was sobering ourselves for an awkward moment before plunging back into the depths of drunkenness. Somewhere around ten that night, we finally stumbled to the car and headed north to Fayetteville.

When we reached Jackson, Mississippi, we stopped for breakfast. My stomach felt like hell, but still slightly better than my head. We reached Fayetteville at six the next morning, hardly time for a shower before I had to take a final test at eight.

Do not ask me how, but I aced the test, perhaps the best score I ever had in grad school. A few months later, Gail and I moved to Oklahoma City and never saw Toni and Terrence again. I have often thought about that Mardi Gras, my lost friendship and failed marriage. Maybe it is because youth is a strange encumbrance whose weight you never really feel until long after Father Time finally removes it.

Eric Wilder

Dr. M's Cattle Ranch

Harvey raised cattle and had a small pasture behind his house in Chalmette where he ran a few head. He had an old friend, a doctor that had a large cattle ranch in the northeastern Louisiana town of Vidalia. Dr. M became very wealthy when a company found oil, and lots of it on his ranch. Shortly after the discovery of black gold, Dr. M retired from medicine and spent his days trading stocks on an old ticker tape machine, and traveling. He was a devout Catholic and the Pope once granted him and his family a private meeting during a visit to the Vatican. Dr. M was also a member of the Krewe of Rex and once paid a million dollars for the privilege of being King of that Krewe during Mardi Gras.

Wanting to experiment with different breeds of cattle, Dr. M hired his old friend Harvey to oversee the operation. Relishing the challenge, Harvey and Lily began splitting their time between Vidalia and Chalmette. On a trip to Chalmette, Gail and I stopped along the way for a visit to the ranch. Dr. M and his family rarely visited so Lily and Harvey had the main house all to themselves. The living room had a large mirror on one wall made of one-way glass. Dr. M was apparently a voyeur and liked watching his guests from an adjacent room that most knew nothing about.

The ranch encompassed two full sections of land and abutted the levee on the west side of the Mississippi River. Harvey and Dr. M were trying to establish a new breed of cattle for the area—Black Angus. The weather turned out too hot and humid for the mostly cooler-weather cows and the experiment ultimately ended in failure.

The ranch had a bunkhouse large enough to accommodate a dozen hired hands, if needed. During our visit there was no seasonal help and Gail and I had the bunkhouse to ourselves. We spent the day touring the ranch, examining barns, stalls and cutting pens. Lily seemed unhappy when we left the following morning and I felt sure she missed her large family in Chalmette.

Perhaps Harvey was also missing home and his own cows because shortly after our visit, he quit his job as foreman and he and Lily moved back to Chalmette for good. Gail and I were glad to see Lily happy again, but I am also thankful that we had the chance to see Dr. M's large working cattle ranch before Harvey finally quit it.

Lily's Squash and Sausage Casserole

Lily and Harvey had their own garden in Chalmette and grew their own produce. Along with tomatoes and mirlitons, they also raised carrots, beans and squash. Lily's fresh Louisiana vegetables made her culinary creations even better. Hey, and yes this is a Cajun dish.

Directions

- 2 pounds squash
- 1 small chopped onion
- 3 tablespoons butter
- ¼ ground sausage
- Cracker crumbs
- Water

Directions

In a skillet mix squash, chopped onion, sausage and a small amount of water. Cook until squash and onions are tender. Brown sausage and then combine with squash and onions. Season to taste with salt and pepper.

Lily's Little Cajun Cookbook

Transfer to 1 quart greased casserole. Cover with cracker crumbs and cook at 350 degrees in oven until brown. Enjoy.

Lily's Seafood Stock

Lily always prepared her own seafood stock. Her method is simple and makes about 2 ½ quarts. Place about 2 pounds fish heads and/or bones and/or shrimp shells in a large pot with some trimmings from onions, celery and carrots in 3 quarts water, or enough to cover. Bring to a boil and simmer 35 to 45 minutes. Strain.

Lily's Oyster Stew

Oyster stew is a Louisiana staple, but is prepared and eaten everywhere the succulent sea creature is found. Like gumbo, there are many variations, some heartier than others. Here is one of Lily's versions.

Ingredients

- 1 stick butter
- 1 tablespoon minced garlic
- 1 medium onion, finely chopped
- 1 medium carrot, finely diced
- 2 tablespoons Cajun seasoning, plus more to taste
- 2 pints oysters, drained and liquor reserved
- 1 quart seafood stock
- 1 10-ounce can of tomatoes, pureed
- 1 quart half-and-half
- ¼ cup white wine or brandy
- Garlic croutons

Directions

In a large 2-gallon stockpot, melt butter over medium-high heat. Add garlic, onion and carrot and cook, stirring constantly, until onions are translucent. Add 2 tablespoons Cajun seasoning and stir to combine. Add oyster liquor, seafood stock and tomatoes and bring to a simmer. Cook 10 minutes. Add half-and-half and bring back to a simmer. Add oysters and cook until their edges begin to curl. Add wine or brandy and adjust seasoning to taste. Serve immediately in hot soup bowls garnished with croutons, green onions, parsley and paprika.

Lily's Oyster Dressing

Lily loved oysters and used them in almost everything she cooked, including the Thanksgiving turkey.

Ingredients

- 3 dozen oysters
- 1 quart stale bread, wet and squeezed
- 2 tablespoons butter
- 1 onion, chopped
- 1 tablespoon parsley
- 1 sprig thyme
- 1 bay leaf
- 3 tablespoons sage
- Salt and pepper to taste

Directions

Drain the oysters, carefully removing all bits of shell. Save oyster liquor for stuffing. Wet the stale bread with hot water, squeezing thoroughly. Mix and season with sage. Chop fowl's liver and gizzard finely, and put 1 tablespoon butter into frying pan. Mix in chopped onion, and chopped liver and gizzard in the pan. As the mixture browns, add the herbs, and then the bread. Mix well. Add remaining butter and stir, blending thoroughly. Add the oyster liquor, and then mix in the oysters. Stir for several minutes before using it to stuff the fowl

Lily's Little Cajun Cookbook

Lily's Steamed Oysters

Lily was a church-going lady and I don't think a drop of liquor ever crossed her lips. Still, she loved to cook and she loved to entertain. When members of her large family dropped by—an everyday occurrence—she would often steam up a batch of oysters. Whenever all of her sons and daughters, sisters and brother, and all their kids were around, there was always a party. Here is her simple, yet wonderful recipe for party time in south Louisiana.

Ingredients

- 4 dozen oysters
- 1 tablespoons butter
- Salt and pepper to taste
- Dash cayenne

Directions

Drain the oysters in their shells and put them in a steamer over a pot of boiling water. Cover and steam for ten minutes. Place in a hot dish and season with salt, pepper and cayenne. Serve with drawn butter sauce and eat while very hot to enjoy the entire flavor.

Midnight on the Bayou

Gail, the youngest member of her family, had seven siblings— five sisters and two brothers. I loved her entire family but my favorites were Clora—the sister closest to Gail's age—and Clora's husband Dennis. Gail had a colorful family, all very intelligent. Clora had an accounting degree, husband Dennis a Master's in mathematics from New Orleans University. Dennis worked for IBM at the Michoud NASA facility. He was good at everything and hated to lose at anything. We had a standing pool match that continued whenever Gail and I came to town. Dennis rarely lost.

Gail and Clora's oldest brother Sonny drove trucks, big semis all around the country. I knew that he liked to drink but learned this in spades when he stopped to visit Gail and me in Oklahoma City. He never appeared drunk, but he kept a vodka-filled flask at all times and started the morning by lacing his coffee with the colorless spirit. His drinking normally didn't affect me until a certain trip Gail and I made to Chalmette.

I grew up north of the state's center. As I have mentioned, several distinct differences mark north and south Louisiana. Most of the original immigrants to south Louisiana were French or Spanish with Catholic being the dominant religion. Many of the original immigrants to north Louisiana were English, most practicing a form of Protestantism. These were not the only differences.

When visiting friends or family in north Louisiana, coffee or iced tea is the hospitality beverage of choice. In south Louisiana it is more commonly a drink of the alcoholic type. Because of this little factoid, it seemed I was rarely sober when I visited Chalmette. It didn't really matter because no one else was sober either. Chalmette is in St. Bernard, a parish surrounded on the south by the Mississippi River and by Bayou Bienvenue to the north. Sonny was a Parish volunteer. As such, he sometimes captained the rescue boat docked at the berth where Paris Road crosses Bayou Bienvenue.

"I'm going to take everyone for a moonlight cruise," he announced one night as we sat in Lily's kitchen.

Most of the family was in town for some holiday or other. In addition to Gail, Clora, Dennis and me, next oldest sister Barbara and her daughter Lynn were in from Houston. Barbara, like all the sisters, was attractive and intelligent. She was a nurse-anesthetist on the DeBakey-Cooley heart transplant team at one of the hospitals in Houston. She worked closely with some of the doctors that pioneered the procedure.

Harvey and Lily always went to sleep with the chickens. The rest of us were ready for a little fun so we piled into a couple of vehicles and headed up Paris Road to Bayou Bienvenue. It was well after dark; the only person sober among us was Lynn who everyone, for some unknown reason, called Lulu. The parish rescue boat was large, thirty feet or so long, and heavy. It was a Gulf-ready boat, capable of sailing through high waves. Despite Sonny's promise, there was no moonlight that night. The center of Bayou Bienvenue is the boundary between the parishes of Orleans and St. Bernard. It crosses the Intracoastal Waterway that leads into shallow Lake Borgne. Shortly into our trip, we learned it was littered with cypress trees, sunken boats and every manner of floating obstacles, none marked whatsoever. It didn't matter because Clora, Barbara, Gail, Dennis and I had brought along alcoholic beverages and were enjoying the ride, despite the fact that we could see nothing but darkness, and a few distant stars. An hour or so passed and it never dawned on us that we should be concerned—at least until Lulu joined us with a report.

"Uncle Sonny is lost. He doesn't have a clue where we are."

We spent the next hour or so motoring through darkness, our alcoholic beverages rapidly depleting, along with our optimism. Dennis and Lulu joined Sonny at the helm to assist. I remained behind to commiserate with Gail, Clora and Barbara. I don't know how he did it, but Dennis somehow managed to steer the behemoth back to its dock, landing it without as much as a scratch.

Gail and I divorced many years ago, a good thing for both of us. Still, I miss her wonderful family and the adventures we had along the way. I never beat Dennis at a single thing the entire time I knew him. Thinking back to that night on Bayou Bienvenue, I feel a little better because I realize just how savvy he was. I don't know if he was somehow responsible for getting the first man on the moon, but I suspect he was present and had a steady hand on the helm.

Lily's Dirty Rice Dressing

Dirty rice is a Cajun specialty and often served as a side dish. Here is Lily's version.

Ingredients

- 1 cup rice
- 1 clove garlic, chopped
- 1 pound ground meat
- Salt, pepper and hot sauce to taste
- 1 pound ground giblets
- Pinch of thyme and sweet basil
- 1 cup chopped onion
- 1 bunch green onions and tops chopped
- ½ cups bell pepper, chopped
- 1 tablespoon parsley, minced
- ½ cup celery, chopped
- 1/4 pound butter

Directions

Cook rice in double boiler until fluffy, using enough salted water to 1 inch above rice. Allow to cook unstirred until all water is gone. In one skillet, sauté ground meat and giblets in butter until brown. In another skillet sauté onions, pepper, celery and seasoning in butter. Add other ingredients. In large pan, mix all above ingredients well, using natural gravy from fowl to moisten.

Eric Wilder

Riding Rodan

Gail loved horses and owned two, Lady, a very gentle mare and Rodan, a large reddish-brown stallion, named for a fictional Japanese monster. His moniker somehow fit him. Not very friendly, Rodan did not tolerate fools and he certainly didn't like carrying one around on his back—a fact I quickly learned during my first visit to Gail's home in Chalmette.

Sprawling Chalmette felt like a family place. Gail's father had a small working ranch right in the middle of town, right across the street from the Chalmette Battlefield, and ran a few horses and some cows. He also bought fur from the many trappers that worked the swamps and marshes south of New Orleans.

Ripley's Believe it or Not featured one of Harvey's cows. It had a tail growing out of its head. Harvey was very proud of the cow and never failed to show visitors his yellowed newspaper clipping. I had not ridden a horse since my brother Jack and I fell off the back of my grandmother's plow horse named Buck. Buck was so large no saddle would fit him. Although not as big, nor as friendly as Buck, Rodan was no small horse. His size did not really matter because I had maintained an aversion to riding horses ever since falling off Buck.

Gail and I met at college in Monroe. On my first trip to meet her parents, I strived to do everything I could to please her and to make a good impression on her family. Because of my desire to present myself in the best possible light, I rashly agreed to go for a ride on Rodan. It was a decision that almost ended our fledgling romance prematurely.

Horses are perceptive animals and Rodan knew the moment that I threw my leg over his back that I was a complete and utter novice. Still, I was okay until Gail handed me the reins. When she did, Rodan took off like a thoroughbred coming out of the gate at Pimlico. The big red horse headed straight for the St. Bernard Highway, congested with traffic even in those days. I could do little except pull on the reins and yell "Whoa, Rodan," at the top of my lungs. My life passed before my eyes as we approached the crowded highway at what felt to me like breakneck speed.

I contemplated jumping but never got the chance. Rodan skidded to an abrupt halt just before plowing into the two lanes heavy traffic. Gail reached us shortly, grabbing his reins and allowing me to exit the saddle as quickly as I could. Neither of us spoke on the short walk back to Harvey's ranch.

Years have passed since that visit and I wish that I could proclaim that it was my last frightening ride on a horse. Well it wasn't. Gail's brother Larry goaded me into another horse ride sometime later. The result was much the same, even though Larry's horse was supposedly a friendly and docile mare. Sensing my discomfort, she ran me beneath a tree, all but knocking my head off on a low branch.

My new wife Marilyn and her three kids own at least six horses. None of them is as big or mean as Rodan was, but it makes no difference to me. Horses and I do not get along and it will be a cold day in Chalmette before I mount another.

Lily's Little Cajun Cookbook

Lily's Crawfish Pie

Yes, fans of Hank Williams, there really is a Cajun dish called crawfish pie. Here is Lily's version.

Ingredients

- 3 cups cooked crawfish, tails and fat
- 1 can cream of mushroom soup
- 3 cups cooked rice
- 4 yolks hard boiled eggs
- 1 ¼ cups of water
- 2 or 3 slices, well buttered bread
- ¼ cup minced celery
- Olive oil or other shortening
- ½ small green pepper, minced
- Salt, black pepper
- Tabasco sauce
- Worcestershire sauce
- Paprika
- Pimientos
- 1 bunch shallots, chopped fine

- 1 bay leaf

Directions

Sauté in olive oil or other shortening, celery, shallots and sweet pepper, about five minutes. Add crawfish tails and fat, sauté about 5 minutes longer. Salt and pepper to taste. Add a few dashes of Tabasco sauce. Mix this with cooked rice; add water, mushroom soup, bay leaf. Add a few dashes of Worcestershire sauce. Test for salt and pepper. Pour entire mixture into a greased baking dish. Grate egg yolks on the top. Remove the crust from the slices of bread, cut each slice into four triangles. Arrange triangles in a circle on top of mixture. Sprinkle with paprika. Bake uncovered in a 350 degree oven for about 30 minutes, until mixture is thoroughly heated and bread is toasted. Garnish with pimientos.

Lily's Crawfish Etouffee

One of the favorite dishes served in the Big Easy is etouffee, made with either shrimp or crawfish. There are as many variations of this dish as there are Cajun cooks. Here is Lily's version:

Ingredients

- ½-cup cooking oil
- 2 cups finely chopped white onion
- 1 large bell pepper, medium diced
- 1 stalk of celery, medium diced
- 2 cups whole tomatoes, mashed
- 2 cups tomato juice
- 1/4 cup lemon juice
- 6 tablespoons roux
- 2 tablespoons Worcestershire
- 1/4 cup minced parsley
- ½ cup chopped leaf of garlic, or green onion tops
- 2 cloves of minced garlic

- 1/4 tablespoon of red pepper
- 1/4 tablespoon of salt, or to taste
- 1/4 tablespoon of pepper, or to taste
- 1 pound of cleaned and de-veined crawfish

Directions

Pour oil into a heavy skillet and sauté onions, bell pepper, and celery until limp. Do not overcook. Add tomatoes, tomato juice, lemon juice, roux and Worcestershire. Bring to a boil, then reduce to medium heat and add parsley, garlic leaf, garlic cloves, red pepper, and salt and pepper. Cook for about five minutes, then add crawfish and cook for fifteen more minutes. Simmer until ready to serve. Over rice, this dish serves four.

A Knight at the Ball

Chalmette is a town down St. Bernard Highway from New Orleans that was all but devastated by Hurricanes Rita and Katrina. Gail had two brothers and six sisters. Sister Mertie was married to a drilling contractor named Bobby. There are many Krewes, or clubs, that celebrate Mardi Gras. They range in size from very large to very small, and they come and go based on many different socio-economic reasons. They all have one thing in common: a king and a queen that serve for only one Mardi Gras season. Rex is one of the oldest and largest Krewes and rumor has it that a person only becomes king after donating a million dollars to the organization. I don't know if this is true, but I did know Dr. M, one of the former kings of Rex, and he was a very rich man.

Brother-in-law Bobby was also wealthy, although not nearly enough to reign over Rex. Lucky for him, there was a Krewe, not quite as famous or large, of which he did become king. Many years ago, Bobby and Mertie were crowned king and queen of the Krewe of Arabi. Bobby lauded the position over everyone in the family and to hear him tell it, he may as well have been King of Saudi Arabia.

While not as expensive to attain as King of Rex, being King of Arabi did not come without a price. Bobby, according to family rumor, had paid fifty thousand dollars for the privilege of serving as king. His costume cost twelve thousand dollars, his wife Mertie's twenty five thousand. They had a son and daughter and each of their costumes cost more than five thousand dollars.

Bobby and his immediate family rode on the King's float during the Arabi parade and threw thousands of dollars worth of beads, doubloons and various premium throws to the adoring masses gathered along the parade route. Bobby also bought thousands of dollars worth of alcoholic beverages served at the Arabi Ball. Being sister and brother-in-law, Gail and I had the privilege of sitting at the King's table and drinking his whiskey.

While nowhere as regal or elegant as the Rex Ball, the Arabi Ball was still quite an affair. Bobby was drunk as a skunk, dressed in full costume and mask, and waving his kingly scepter like a royal fool. As the night progressed, he began knighting the male members of his entourage. When my turn arrived, I came close to losing an ear in the process. Bobby did not like me very much, but in deference to Gail's father, he was civil to me when he was sober. The problem was, his sobriety was an unusual occurrence. The night of the Arabi Ball, he was anything but. He didn't even acknowledge my presence as I knelt before him, awaiting knighthood.

The large ballroom was dark, music from a live orchestra loud, along with the noise of restless revelers. No one except Bobby and I realized that instead of the normal knighting, he had struck me with the sword hard enough to knock off my mask and put a bloody gash in my scalp. Okay, I was also drunk having consumed a goodly amount of Bobby's bourbon. Acting as if nothing outside the ordinary had happened, he simply wheeled around on his throne and continued reveling. Yes, Bobby was drunk, the large ballroom dark and noisy. My own mind, and body, was impaired. I really do not know if he struck me in malice or simply let fly a misjudged blow because of his drunken stupor. Quickly forgetting the incident, I cleaned the blood off my head in the bathroom and returned to the raucous party.

I am no longer a member of the family, nor, do I believe, is Bobby. There was no permanent damage done from Bobby's blow—intentional or otherwise. Every knight must face a little adversity, and hey, I am now Sir Eric, Knight of Arabi.

Lily's Beignets

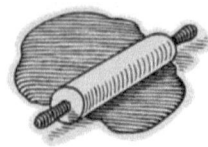

Lily's desserts were to die for. Beignets are like square doughnuts without the hole, and most often associated with the all-night French Quarter must place to visit—Cafe du Monde. Although not quite as famous, Lily's were just as good.

Ingredients

- ½ package yeast cake
- 3 ½ cups flour, plain
- 1cup milk
- ¾ tablespoons salt
- 2 tablespoons sugar
- 1 egg
- 2 tablespoons cooking oil
- Powdered sugar

Directions

Soften yeast cake in 1/3 cup lukewarm water to form a paste. Warm the milk and add sugar, oil and yeast mixture. Gradually stir in 2 cups flour and the salt. Stir

Lily's Little Cajun Cookbook

until it forms a batter. Stir in egg until it is mixed well, and then add rest of flour. Mix well. Cover and set in warm place about 1 ½ hours to rise. Take dough out and roll until about ¼ inch thick. Cut in 2 inch pieces. Place on cookie sheet or pan and let rise another half hour. Fry dough until it is brown and then remove and let drain. Sprinkle with powdered sugar and enjoy.

Lily's Bread Pudding with Rum Sauce

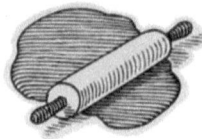

Ingredients

- 1 loaf stale French bread
- ¼ can evaporated milk
- 1 pound butter
- 1 ¼ cups sugar
- ¼ pound raisins
- 1 small can pineapple, crushed
- 3 eggs, beaten
- 3 tablespoons vanilla extract
- ¼ cup brown sugar

Directions

Preheat oven to 350 degrees. Wet the bread and squeeze the water out of it. Melt the butter and mix with all other ingredients. Pour mixture into a well-greased 4 x 10-inch baking pan. Bake for 2 ½ hours. The pudding will rise in the first hour. After an hour, remove pan from oven and stir the mixture to tighten it. Return to the oven for the second hour of cooking.

Rum Sauce

Ingredients

- ¼ stick butter, melted
- 1 cup sugar
- 1 cup flour
- ½ cup rum

Directions

Place all ingredients in double boiler and cook for 10 minutes. Beat until fluffy.

Eric Wilder

Raining Cats and Dogs

A recent spring storm resonating with the sights and sounds of booming thunder and flashing lightning, reminded me of a damp trip Gail and I took to New Orleans, via Vidalia, Louisiana. The time was late winter. Gail and I had finished work at our jobs and decided on a whim to visit her parents in Vidalia before continuing on to Chalmette. The ranch was just across the mighty Mississippi River from Natchez. We planned to spend the night there and then head south for a little respite from our college drudgery.

Darkness had already fallen before we pulled out of our Fayetteville, Arkansas driveway, drops of rain beginning to dampen the windshield. Somewhere in central Arkansas, light rain turned into a serious storm, the wipers on our old 1962 Ford truck barely keeping up with the tempo of the downpour. As we neared the rice fields of southeast Arkansas, the wipers halted altogether. The downpour and our lack of wipers rendered us suddenly sightless and I cautiously pulled the truck to the side of the road until we could assess the mechanical failure. After groping around under the dash, I soon learned that the cause of the malfunction was a missing "C" clamp. We searched on the floor of the truck with the dim illumination of a flashlight with nearly spent batteries but it was to no avail.

Rain continued and we realized that we were either stuck on the side of the road, or we would have to improvise and carry on. Experimenting, I learned that I could manually manipulate the wipers by driving with one hand while using the other to work the mechanism. The storm did anything but abate. Southeastern Arkansas is flat. Very flat! Water poured across the highway in waves and I quickly learned the old saying "raining cats and dogs" was rooted in reality. Fish from the rice fields and drainage ditches flowed across the road in our path. It was quite an experience, steering with one hand while working the wipers with the other, all the while trying to avoid wildlife pouring across the road in front of us.

We finally made it to Vidalia, mostly unscathed. The deluge continued as we said a late goodnight to Gail's parents—after a well-deserved bowl of Lily's gumbo—and claimed a much deserved rest in an empty room in the ranch's rustic bunkhouse.

Lily's Barbecue Shrimp

They don't exactly cook shrimp on the barby in south Louisiana, nor do they slather them in barbecue sauce, as the name implies. Instead, they have a succulent dish that is simply wonderful. Here is Lily's version.

Ingredients

- 1 tablespoon olive oil
- ½ pound smoked hot sausage, sliced
- 1 medium onion, diced
- ½ pound chicken, cubed
- ½ teaspoon Creole seasoning
- 2 cloves garlic, minced
- 1 rib celery, diced
- 1 bell pepper, diced
- 2 cups beef broth
- ¼ teaspoon whole thyme
- 1 cup raw rice

Lily's Little Cajun Cookbook

Directions

Heat oil in a heavy pot. Add sausage and cook on medium heat, stirring occasionally, until browned. Add onion, and brown. Add chicken and Creole seasoning, and cook, stirring occasionally, until chicken browns. Add garlic, celery, bell pepper, broth and thyme and bring to a boil. Add rice, cover, reduce heat, and simmer, stirring occasionally, until liquid is absorbed and rice is tender, about 20 to 25 minutes.

Eric Wilder

Prince of Arabi

I worked in New Orleans during the summer of 1968 and had many adventures, and misadventures, during that time. I lived in Arabi, a community between Chalmette and the Lower 9th Ward. Known for its rampant organized gambling that continued until the 1950s, Arabi barely survived Hurricanes Rita and Katrina.

I resided on the ground floor of a two-storied wood-frame house, just across the street from a Catholic convent. Nuns that went into the convent never came out again, cloistered for life. My little apartment had no air conditioning and reeked of decades of mold and mildew. Oh, and did I mention the cockroaches?

I had a car, a green '67 Ford Mustang, but usually took the bus to work. Gas was not expensive then, or the issue it is now. New Orleans drivers were simply the worst I had ever encountered, at least on this side of the border from Mexico. I usually walked the quarter-mile from my apartment to the bus stop where I would catch the bus to Canal.

I spent a lot of time that summer taking in the nightlife of one of the wildest cities in the world and often catnapped on my way to work, and on my way home. I awoke once at the bus terminal in Arabi to the sight of a young black man pointing a pistol directly at me and the woman sitting beside me. Everyone else had already escaped through the side door. I grabbed the woman and pulled her down behind the seat, knowing that a ricochet would still get us if he fired the pistol.

He didn't get the chance; two men tackled him from behind and wrestled the weapon from his grasp. I walked home that night never learning the reason for the pistol brandishing and too young to realize that I had likely narrowly escaped death.

My brother, also a geology student, got a job with the same company as me before the summer ended. He kept the shabby apartment after I left to return to college. He married a girl that worked with us. They are still married, have four kids and a few grandkids now.

No life remained in the little town when Marilyn and I visited shortly after Katrina's devastation, only signs posted by construction companies offering to raze abandoned houses. The convent across the street where I once lived remained, and I have always wondered if the cloistered nuns had abandoned their posts, or stayed to face the wrath of an angry god.

Lily's Chicken Sauce Piquante

A certain spicy stew is a cooking staple in south Louisiana. Sauce piquante was introduced to Louisiana by the Spanish. It has been embraced by Cajun chefs and has evolved into nearly as many differing recipes as there are cooks. The dish begins with a roux, combined with the sauce and almost any meat you can think of. In Louisiana, there is chicken, pork, wild duck, turtle and even alligator sauce piquante. Here is Lily's version using chicken.

Ingredients

- 1 chicken, cut up
- ¼ cup chopped shallots
- ½ cup cooking oil
- 1 8 ounce cans tomato sauce
- ½ cup flour
- 1 cup water
- 2 large onions, chopped

Lily's Little Cajun Cookbook

- 1 cup Burgundy
- 4 garlic cloves, chopped
- ¼ cup chopped parsley
- 1 medium bell pepper
- Salt, pepper and hot sauce to taste

Directions

Make roux with cooking oil and flour, stirring constantly until medium brown. Add onions, garlic, bell pepper and shallots. Sauté until onions are clear. Add chicken, tomato sauce, water, Burgundy, parsley and seasoning. Cover and cook over medium heat for 30 minutes (stirring occasionally) or until sauce begins to thicken. Serve over rice.

Eric Wilder

Clueless in Chalmette

Harvey was a fur buyer. I was just back from Vietnam, scheduled to start graduate school the next spring. Harvey apparently mistrusted my intentions and assumed that I intended to be a perennial student, and somehow on the dole—his dole. The thought was the furthest thing from my mind, but it seems to be the opinion he and all my other relatives had at the time. He was worried about it enough that he even tried to teach me how to grade fur. Harvey had a shed where he kept his furs before transporting them downtown to the French Market where he ultimately sold them.

"This is a rat fur," he said, pointing to a muskrat skin. "I pay a dollar for a regular pelt and a little more for a grade A pelt. Know how I tell the difference?"

I didn't have a clue. The pelts were turned inside out and he stuck his hand inside one, showing me what to do.

"I pass my hand over the fur to see if there are any bald or thin spots. If there are, the fur isn't worth as much. I always give at least a dollar a pelt or else the trappers would take their furs some place else. If they bring me a hundred rats, I give them at least a hundred dollars. Everything over that amount is a bonus. You understand?"

I nodded to indicate that I did, but I had no idea at the time where the lecture was going.

Gail and I had intended to live with Harvey and Lily for three months, and then three months with my parents before moving to Fayetteville, just before the beginning spring semester. It didn't happen that way. After about a week, they began treating us like bad breath. My sister-in-law even called and offered to pay my way through a real estate course so that Gail and I would stop sponging off their parents. I'm fairly dense, but I was starting to get the hint. That night I had a talk with Gail.

"I can't take much more of this," I said. "Your parents obviously don't want us here."

"But what will we do?"

"Spend the rest of the time with my parents. I think they are more understanding."

Next day we packed and drove to Vivian, Lily crying but not begging us to stay. After a week at my parent's house, we got another rude awakening. They too began treating us like, well like blood-sucking leeches. After just a few days, we packed our bags again and left for Fayetteville.

For the first time in my life I learned that families are strange, really strange. The may love you but they don't want you living with them, or for you to give the rest of the family the impression that you are living off of them.

It was a good lesson but it leaves me with one question—why can't I get rid of my own kids as easily?

Eric Wilder

Lily's Chalmette Meatloaf

Lily was a wonderful cook. Not only could she cook Cajun and Creole dishes, she also knew how to prepare traditional southern dishes, famous from Florida to Texas. Meatloaf, without question, is a southern comfort food, and here is Lily's Creole version of the recipe.

Ingredients

- 2 bay leaves, whole
- 1 tablespoon salt
- 1 teaspoon ground red cayenne pepper
- 1 teaspoon black pepper
- ½ teaspoon cumin, ground
- ½ teaspoon nutmeg, ground
- 4 tablespoons butter, unsalted
- ½ cup of celery, finely chopped
- ½ cup bell pepper, finely chopped
- ¼ cup greens onions, chopped
- 12 teaspoons of garlic, minced
- 1 tablespoon Tabasco sauce
- 1 tablespoon Worcestershire sauce
- ½ cup milk

Lily's Little Cajun Cookbook

- ½ cup catsup
- 2 pounds beef, ground
- ½ pound of pork, ground
- 2 eggs lightly beaten
- 1 cup bread crumbs

Directions

Combine the seasoning mix and ingredients in a small bowl. Set aside. Melt the butter in 1 quart saucepan over medium heat. Add the onions, celery, and bell pepper, green onions, garlic, Tabasco, Worcestershire and seasoning mix. Sauté about 6 minutes, stirring occasionally and scraping the pan bottom well. Stir in the milk and ½ cup catsup. Continue cooking for about 2 minutes, stirring occasionally. Remove from the heat and allow mixture to cool to room temperature. Place the ground beef and pork in an ungreased 13 x 9 inch baking pan. Remove the bay leaves. Add the eggs, the cooked vegetable mixture and the bread crumbs. Mix by hand until thoroughly combined in the center of the pan. Shape the mixture into a loaf that is about 1 ½ inches high x 6 inches wide and 12 inches long. Bake uncovered at 350 for 25 minutes, then raise heat to 400 and continue cooking until done, about 35 minutes longer.

Lily's Rice Dressing

Lily had eight children. All her kids and their families usually came to her house for Thanksgiving, Christmas and Easter. Even though she was French-Acadian, she like families across the country, would usually also cook a traditional turkey, in addition to her wonderful Cajun fare. Here is a recipe for a Cajun dressing she would often serve with it.

Ingredients

- 4 cups chicken or turkey stock
- 2 cups rice
- 1 pound chicken gizzards
- ½ pound chicken livers
- ½ pound ground beef
- ½ pound pork
- ½ cup oil or meat drippings
- 1 large onion, chopped
- 2 stalks celery, chopped
- 1 bell pepper, chopped
- 2 cloves garlic, minced
- 3 tablespoons parsley, chopped

Lily's Little Cajun Cookbook

- 1 bunch green onions, chopped
- Salt, pepper, to taste

Directions

Bring chicken stock to a boil in a large saucepan. Add rice, reduce heat, cover and simmer until done, about 20 minutes. Set aside. Simmer chicken gizzards in water until fork tender, about 30 minutes, add livers and cook about 10 more minutes until livers are done. Drain and remove the tender meat from the gizzards, discarding the tough gristle. Grind or process gizzard meat and livers together until coarse. Set aside.

In a large pot, brown the ground beef and pork, drain and set aside. In the same pot, heat the oil and sauté onions, celery and bell pepper until soft. Add garlic and sauté briefly. Away from the heat, add rice, meat, green onions, parsley and seasonings, and toss lightly.

Lily's Red Fish Chalmette

Red snapper is perhaps the most popular main entrée at many fine restaurants in New Orleans. Lily always prepared a wonderful version she called, simply, red fish. She always made her signature dish when her little brother Junior brought home red snapper from one of his morning fishing trips.

Ingredients

- 2 onions, minced
- 1 sprig saffron
- 2 green peppers, minced
- 4 pounds red snapper
- 2 fresh mushrooms, minced
- 1 cup white wine
- 1 clove garlic, crushed
- Salt and pepper
- 2 tablespoons olive oil
- 1 tablespoon chopped parsley
- 6 fresh tomatoes, peeled

Lily's Little Cajun Cookbook

Directions

Cook onions, peppers, mushrooms and garlic in olive oil for a few minutes, add tomatoes and cook for 30 minutes. Add saffron. Remove head and middle bone from fish and arrange in a buttered baking dish. Pour wine over fish and season very lightly with salt and pepper. Add sauce and cook for 30 minutes in a 350-degree oven. Garnish with parsley.

Lily's Cajun Butter

We all like butter on our corn. Lily used to whip up a special concoction she called Cajun butter and often served it over carrots, cauliflower and even her mirlitons. It makes fresh vegetables taste even more wonderful and it's easy to prepare. Whip up a batch and see if you don't agree.

Ingredients

- 1 tablespoon olive oil
- 2 teaspoon lemon juice
- 1/8 teaspoon parsley
- 1/4 teaspoon chili powder
- 1/4 teaspoon ground black pepper
- 1/8 teaspoon garlic powder
- 1/4 teaspoon ground red pepper
- 2 tablespoon butter
- 1 teaspoon cornstarch
- 1/4 cup chicken broth

Lily's Little Cajun Cookbook

Directions

Mix parsley, chili powder, black pepper, garlic powder and red pepper. Cook in hot butter and olive oil for 1 minute. Stir in cornstarch. Add chicken broth and lemon juice. Cook and stir over medium heat until thickened and bubbly. Cook and stir 2 minutes more. Serve warm over corn or vegetables.

Eric Wilder

Lily's Famous Eggplant Dressing

The best Cajun cook I ever knew was my former mother-in-law Lily. Every meal was an experience and always served up in authentic fashion. One of my favorite side dishes was her famous eggplant dressing that she prepared, like all her other culinary creations, sans cookbook.

Ingredients

- 2 large purple eggplants, cubed and diced
- 5 slices of bacon
- ¾ pound ground pork
- 1 ½ teaspoons black pepper
- Salt to taste
- 1 large cans whole tomatoes
- 2 ½ cups cooked rice
- French bread crumbs
- 1 ½ cups onion, garlic, sweet pepper, chopped

Lily's Little Cajun Cookbook

Directions

Cook the eggplants in salted water until soft. Drain, mash and set aside. Sauté bacon in large cast-iron skillet and then add onion, garlic and sweet pepper mixture. Sauté until vegetables are wilted and then add to eggplants. Cook the ground pork until brown, drain the fat and then stir in the eggplant mixture. Add the can of tomatoes, salt and pepper and bread crumbs. Mix well and then simmer on medium-low heat for about twenty minutes. Pour the mixture into a casserole dish, add the rice and more bread crumbs and then bake at 350 degrees for thirty minutes. Enjoy.

Eric Wilder

Harvey's Diet Tip

I love south Louisiana cooking and my former mother-in-law Lily was possibly the best Cajun-Creole cook there ever was. She had several sisters and a younger brother. Except for the three youngest daughter's, all of her children and all of her siblings lived within a few miles radius. It goes without saying that there is nothing more important to a person from south Louisiana than their family, and anytime Gail and I made it back to Chalmette it was cause for celebration.

I grew up in north Louisiana. The people there are just as friendly but they are more likely to serve coffee to their guests than whiskey. In addition, you were more likely to get hash browns for breakfast instead of grits. Harvey and Lily were teetotalers and drank no alcoholic beverages at all. They also frowned on those that did. Still, they were the only members of the family that felt that way. Whenever Gail and I knocked on the door of an aunt, uncle or cousin, there was always a drink—as in alcoholic—waiting for us on the other side.

Everyone in the family was a great cook and they all enjoyed drinking and eating. It didn't seem to matter because there wasn't a single fat person in the entire family. Except for my particularly obnoxious ex-brother-in-law, I don't recall anyone ever drinking more alcohol than they could cope with. Unfortunately, I've never possessed either seemingly inbred talent. I've had to fight my waistline all my life. Harvey must have noticed because one evening we were alone and he called me over to the kitchen table. He was drinking Lily's strong Cajun coffee and I joined him, waiting anxiously to hear the reason he wanted to talk to me.

"When I was a young man, I had a problem with my weight," he said. I had to listen carefully because Harvey always spoke in a voice so low that you had to hang on his every word. Perhaps that was his design.

"My doctor gave me a bit of advice." He said, "Harvey, no matter how good the food tastes, only eat one helping and when you are finished always have desert, a little something sweet to tell your brain that the meal is over. You might try it sometime. It works."

That was Harvey's diet tip. Enjoy your food but do not have seconds, and always have desert. His advice for eating works. I only wish he were still alive to tell me how to fool my brain into thinking that I don't need just one more beer.

Eric Wilder

Culture, Cuisine and Killer Hurricanes—and now Oil Spills

I'd like to end this little cookbook on a somber note, not because that's Lily's or the Chalmette way, but because it deserves to be said. I think Lily would agree.

With New Orleans in the bull's eye of approaching hurricanes, it is important to remember what a national treasure the City is. Although founded by the French, many other nationalities have combined to shape the Big Easy's diverse culture. I'm not going out on a limb when I say that no other geographical setting has influenced the cuisine of the Nation, and the world as has New Orleans. Wonderful food isn't the only remarkable thing about the city. No other location in our nation has experienced such a diverse combination of cultures as has the Big Easy and this has resulted in an extraordinary mixture of language, art, music, literature, and architecture.

Truly the jewel of the Gulf Coast, New Orleans is in a broad region that is critically important to the rest of the nation because of proximity to this country's largest single source of oil and gas, along with its tourism, shipping and refining.

Hurricane Katrina critically injured New Orleans. Many parts of the City remain much the same as they were days after that horrible storm. It is sad that many of the problems exposed by Katrina and Rita—primarily a deficient levee system—remain uncorrected. Now the Gulf Coast is assailed by yet another disaster—a wild offshore oil well blowing out sixty thousand barrels of oil a day. Will New Orleans, Louisiana and the Gulf Coast survive? Yes, but not without our help.

End

Born near fabled Black Bayou in northwest Louisiana, Eric Wilder began writing during a career as a petroleum geologist. He now lives in Edmond, Oklahoma, and still searches for elusive black gold when he isn't writing a new mystery. Please visit him at EricWilder.com.

www.ingramcontent.com/pod-product-compliance
Lightning Source LLC
Chambersburg PA
CBHW031302290426
44109CB00012B/683